BEST EDITORIAL CARTOONS OF THE YEAR

1976 EDITION

Edited by

CHARLES BROOKS

Foreword by Blaine

PELICAN PUBLISHING COMPANY

GRETNA 1976

Copyright © 1976
By Charles G. Brooks
All rights reserved
ISBN: 0-88289-122-7
LCN: 74-29707
First printing

Cataloging in Publication Data

Library of Congress Catalog Card Number: 74-29707

Brooks, Charles
        Best Editorial Cartoons of the Year:
1976 Edition, 4th Edition
Gretna, Louisiana   Pelican Pub. Co.
June, 1976
        4th book in a series of annuals.

Manufactured in the United States of America

Published by Pelican Publishing Company, Inc.
630 Burmaster Street, Gretna, Louisiana 70053

Designed by Barney McKee

Contents

Foreword

I am convinced that good caricature adds a special value to editorial cartoons, either as a vehicle to the main point of the cartoon itself, or as a means of underscoring it. I am equally certain that readers develop a more sustained interest in editorial cartoons when they are amused by the humor and rendering of a clever caricature, particularly on a day when the basic idea may not be one of the best.

There are so many excellent cartoonists in the Association of American Editorial Cartoonists that I am delighted to be a part of a book such as this which enables me to maintain an updated view on the recent works of my colleagues.

It is refreshing to see such a variety of styles and interpretations of the same characters by so many cartoonists. Caricature represents one of the few remaining qualities of modern life that adheres to a genuine principle of individuality. Although reflecting some influence by his favorite predecessors, each cartoonist maintains a unique style in his execution of a subject that becomes as personal as his signature.

When a reader sees a caricature of some politician who is ripping him off with taxes, for example, he may experience a vicarious pleasure by imagining that he would draw the individual the same way—that is, if he could draw.

Technically, good caricature comes only from years of practice—and from a willingness to redraw everything that does not measure up. One gradually develops an eye for the important features to accentuate in a face, along with a knowledge of the degrees of distortion. Eventually, one finds he has developed his own special style.

Experts such as Al Hirshfield, the great theatre caricaturist, have mastered an unusual, highly simplified line approach to caricature. Every line is obviously carefully planned, and any apparent ease of execution comes only from having developed a second nature through repetition.

On the other hand, a young Parisian cartoonist, Jean Mulatier, once told me he devoted as much as three weeks to complete one caricature. And not because he is a slow worker. His superbly detailed renderings, in color, are genuine works of art, but nevertheless still liberally distorted caricatures.

I tend to work between both of these approaches, occasionally leaning more toward one than the other. The caricatures I consider my best are extremely loose, yet controlled brush and ink lines reflecting simplicity, but they are given the appearance of being quite detailed by a casual rounding out of the main forms using thin, short hatch-lines. All this can be done meticulously or rapidly when sketching someone in person.

FOREWORD

In preparing my daily cartoons, I usually tape seven to fifteen photographs of the subject to my drawing board to give me a general view of the task ahead. Often I draw a preliminary sketch to get "the look" in mind. Then I loosen up on a second drawing. Sometimes I draw directly in brush and ink without previous pencil work. That turns out to look more naturally loose, but requires maximum confidence. After I complete the caricature portion, I then draw the rest of the cartoon around it. Often the subjects I draw can be completed without the aid of photographs.

Fellow cartoonists have suggested that I have a knack for spotting

features about a face beyond the obvious features that many cartoonists may exaggerate, and that my flair for expression combines to give my caricatures a more striking resemblance. Eric Seidman, art director of the New York *Times*, paid me, as a caricaturist, the supreme compliment when he said: "I find something in your sketches that is truly artistic. Obviously you keep a needle point on your brush. Your caricature of Mao, for instance, almost approaches fine art. It doesn't approach it . . . it is!"

The point I want to make here is that I don't have to be aware that it is a caricature of Mao, nor do I have to know that it is of someone who really exists. I simply liked that particular cartoon as a drawing. The fact that it is of an important world figure merely enhances its impact. The caricature of Sammy Davis, Jr., on this page underscores this point.

I believe my colleagues have done an excellent job of caricaturing "the bland Mr. Ford," in spite of their earlier doubts. I believe the

public is beginning to identify with what the President actually looks like by the cartoons they have seen, rather than by the bland news photos.

Perhaps I should emphasize that neither my fellow cartoonists nor I could draw President Ford effectively in our first few attempts. The more even-featured the subject is—and President Ford does have rather even features—the more difficult he is to caricature. But that poses little threat to caricaturists. The world is full of characters, as anyone might observe in any large crowd. In fact, a crowd of cartoonists at their own convention is a mass of walking cartoons.

President Ford and Prime Minister Trudeau would be delighted, I am sure, if they saw the caricatures we do of each other at these events.

Caricature is a unique art that has been mastered by so many cartoonists and has become such an attraction in editorial cartoons that I feel it should be given consideration as a separate category in exhibitions and award presentations. In the meantime, I speak for my colleagues when I say that we are grateful to the publisher for this series on the complete editorial cartoon. It is a positive reality that includes a generous share of outstanding caricature.

Blaine

The Spectator   CANADA

Award-Winning Cartoons

1975 PULITZER PRIZE

GARRY TRUDEAU

Editorial Cartoonist
Universal Press Syndicate

Born 1949; graduate of the Yale Art School; columnist; co-founder and editor of tri-lingual magazine for the Washington, D.C., diplomatic corps; regarded as innovator of new genre of political and social commentary; creator of cartoon strip, Doonesbury; nine collections of Doonesbury have been published in book form.

1974 NATIONAL NEWSPAPER AWARD/CANADA

(Selected in 1975)

BLAINE

Editorial Cartoonist
Hamilton (Ont.) Spectator

Born Cape Breton, Canada; editorial cartoonist, *Toronto Globe and Mail, The Spectator*; first winner of the Salon of Cartoons, Montreal; only Canadian to win Reuben Award for cartooning; author of two books of cartoons; portrait commissions include Robert and John F. Kennedy; holds black belt in karate; syndicated by Miller Services of Toronto.

1974 SIGMA DELTA CHI AWARD

(Selected in 1975)

" I'VE FOUND THE PERFECT JUROR YOUR HONOR....., NEVER HEARD OF WATERGATE....
..DOESN'T KNOW OF ANYONE INVOLVED..... HASN'T READ A PAPER OR WATCHED T.V. IN YEARS....."

MIKE PETERS

Editorial Cartoonist
Dayton Daily News

Born 1943 in St. Louis, Mo.; graduate of fine arts, Washington University; cartoonist for *Chicago Defender*, 1966, *Okinawa Morning Star*, 1967-68, *Chicago Daily News*, 1969, and *Dayton Daily News*, 1969 to the present; syndicated by United Features.

1975 NATIONAL HEADLINERS
CLUB AWARD

'How's that bullet sandwich, kid?'

BILL SANDERS

Editorial Cartoonist
Milwaukee Journal

Editorial cartoonist and sports writer, *Stars and Stripes*, Tokyo, 1957-59; editorial cartoonist, Greensboro, North Carolina, *Daily News*, 1959-63, *Kansas City Star*, 1963-67, *Milwaukee Journal*, 1967 to the present; presented special service award by Wisconsin Civil Liberties Union, 1972; cartoons syndicated by Publisher-Hall Syndicate.

Best Editorial Cartoons of the Year

The Ford Administration

Using the veto thirty-two times during the year, President Gerald Ford managed to preserve many of his policies from a predominantly Democratic Congress. The Democrats could override only four of his vetoes, even failing to reverse his veto of an important bill tightening controls on strip mining. Ford maintained that his vetoes were necessary to keep a lid on the wild spending of congressional liberals.

By appointing Judge John Paul Stephens to succeed retired U.S. Supreme Court Justice William O. Douglas, Ford avoided controversy. A moderately conservative jurist, Stephens was expected to join swing justices Byron White and Potter Stewart in most of his decisions.

Travel seemed to appeal to the President during the year, so much so that it threatened to become a campaign issue in 1976.

In a surprise reshuffling of his key advisors, Ford created a storm of protests by firing Secretary of Defense James Schlesinger, CIA Director William Colby, and Secretary of Commerce Rogers C. B. Morton. Donald Rumsfeld, George Bush, and Elliott Richardson were then named to the posts, respectively.

MIKE PETERS
Courtesy Dayton Daily News

"FROM NOW ON I USE ONLY GENUINE FORD PARTS!"

CHARLES WERNER
Courtesy Indianapolis Star

"I'M THE PRESIDENT, AND HE SAYS YOU'RE FIRED!"

JOHN STAMPONE
Courtesy Army Times

CLYDE WELLS
Courtesy Augusta (Ga.) Chronicle

JON KENNEDY
Courtesy Arkansas Democrat

JOHN LANE
©NEA

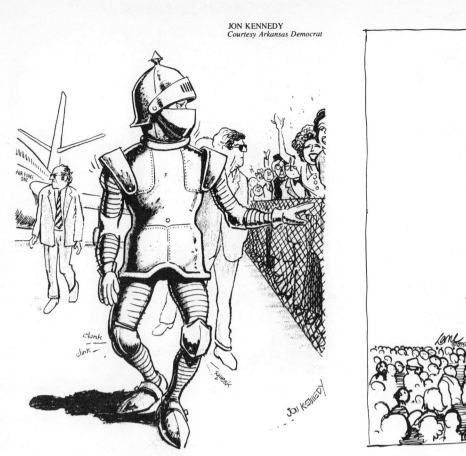

'76 model Ford?

"You mean they're *all* security guards?"

ED HINRICHS
Courtesy Madison Capital Times

"Mama, if this guy'd been with Custer, he wouldn't have seen no indians!!"

Speaking Of Bankruptcy

*"I should think, Mr. President, that your bulletproof
vest would prove sufficient."*

Gift For Future Generations

DICK LOCHER
Courtesy Chicago Tribune

GENE BASSET
Courtesy Scripps-Howard Newspapers

"CONGRATS... WE'RE BACK IN THE BIG TIME, CHAMP!"

"CHARGE!"

FEDERAL SPENDING

—By BOB TAYLOR, Times Herald Staff Cartoonist
BOB TAYLOR
Courtesy Dallas Times Herald

ED ASHLEY
Courtesy Toledo Blade

WAYNE STAYSKAL
Courtesy Chicago Tribune

"BOY, WAIT'LL I TELL THE GANG I SHOOK HANDS WITH THE PRESIDENT!"

"NOW THAT'S WHAT I CALL A DO-SOMETHING PRESIDENT—ALREADY THIS MORNING HE'S VETOED HALF OF HIS ENGLISH MUFFIN, TWO CANDID PHOTOS BY SUSAN, AND THE EDITORIAL PAGE OF THE WASHINGTON POST"

© 1975 by NEA, Inc.

JIM BERRY
©NEA

"This is like eating peanuts! Bring me more bills to veto!"

"HE'S BEGINNING TO GET MY ATTENTION"

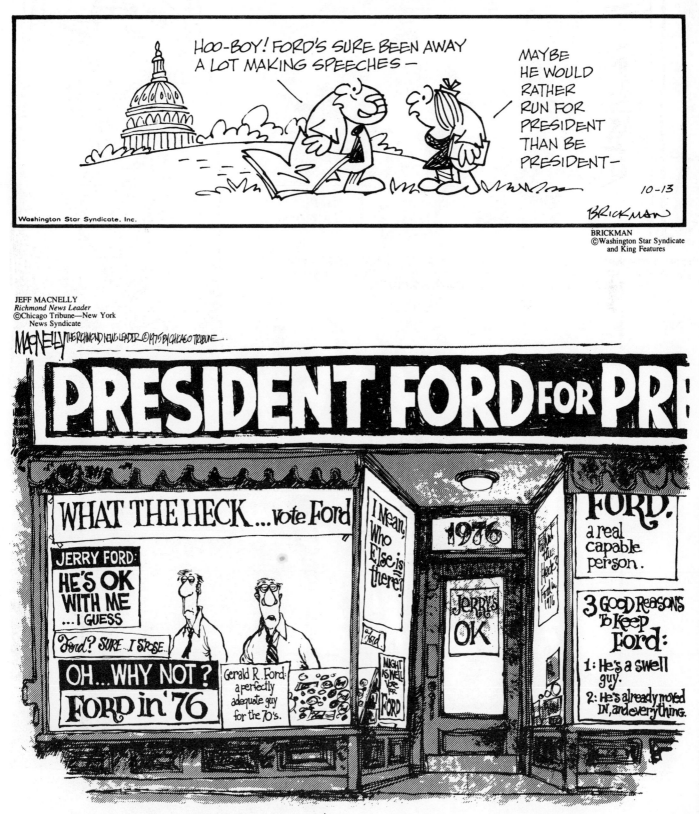

BRICKMAN
©Washington Star Syndicate
and King Features

JEFF MACNELLY
Richmond News Leader
©Chicago Tribune—New York
News Syndicate

"DO YOU GET THE FEELING THIS CAMPAIGN LACKS A LITTLE SOMETHING?"

STATE OF THE UNION

BEN SARGENT
Courtesy Austin American

"Who WAS that masked man?"

"...and, then, with the Alan Greenspan Chorus in the background, singing, 'For He's a Jolly Good Fellow'...."

THE GERALD FORD ECONOMIC ROAD SHOW

BILL GRAHAM
Arkansas Gazette

HE GOT CARRIED AWAY

WARREN KING
Courtesy N.Y. Daily News

JERRY DOYLE
Courtesy Philadelphia Daily News

CHARLES BISSELL
Courtesy Nashville Tennessean

"—Because it could get in your way when your leg's well . . . See?"

"OF COURSE I HAVE MALPRACTICE INSURANCE — WHY DO YOU ASK?"

ED ASHLEY
Courtesy Toledo Blade

"BLESSINGS ON THEE, LITTLE MAN—"

LOU GRANT
Oakland Tribune
©Los Angeles Times Syndicate

Presidential Hopefuls

There was no shortage of contenders for the Democratic nomination for President at the July, 1976, convention. The party's liberal wing was represented early by Representative Morris Udall of Arizona, former senator Fred Harris of Oklahoma, Senator Birch Bayh of Indiana, Governor Milton Shapp of Pennsylvania, Terry Sanford, former governor of North Carolina, Jimmy Carter, former governor of Georgia, and Sargent Shriver of Massachusetts. Moderates in the running included Senator Henry Jackson of Washington and Senator Lloyd Bentsen of Texas. At year's end, however, Alabama's George Wallace appeared strongest in delegate strength.

Many longtime observers were betting that Senator Hubert Humphrey of Minnesota would emerge from a deadlocked convention with the nomination.

On November 20 Ronald Reagan declared his long-expected candidacy for the Republican nomination, assuring incumbent Ford a strong challenge for the party's top prize.

DWANE POWELL
Courtesy Cincinnati Enquirer

'It's a special pickup for pickin' up th' Democratic nomination . . .'

ZSCHIESCHE
KING FEATURES
BOB ZSCHIESCHE
©King Features

HUGH HAYNIE
Louisville Courier-Journal
©Los Angeles Times Syndicate

CHUCH HAYNIE ©1975 The Courier-Journal   DISTRIBUTED BY L. A. TIMES SYNDICATE

"Okay . . . are there any other Democratic presidential candidates who'd like t'be in the group picture?"

BALDY
Courtesy Atlanta Constitution

Louisville Courier-Journal
©Los Angeles Times Syndicate

"...I MAY USE YOU IN A BIT PART FOR A FORTHCOMING TORRID LOVE SCENE!"

JEFF MACNELLY
Richmond News Leader
©Chicago Tribune—New York
  News Syndicate

"OKAY, MR. CONNALLY, SHE'S MOVING OUT OF THE WAY.... MR. CONNALLY?....ARE YOU STILL IN THERE?...."

BYRON HUMPHREY
Courtesy New Orleans States-Item

YES, HE WILL

NO, HE WON'T

TIP AND TEDDY

"I see a compromise coming...you're running your top fifteen contenders as a committee...!"

GEE___IT'S GETTING VERY LATE___ DO YOU REALLY THINK REAGAN WILL SHOW UP?

DON'T WORRY__HE'S FAMOUS FOR LATE SHOWS__

REAGAN FOR PRESIDENT

"How do I know he's going to run? Because he denies it even when no one asks him."

Rockefeller

On November 3, Vice-President Nelson Rockefeller delivered a letter to President Ford which declared: "I do not wish my name to enter into your consideration for the upcoming Republican vice-presidential nomination." Thus, after ten months and fourteen days as the President's understudy, Rockefeller succumbed to pressure from the party's conservative wing to remove himself from contention.

It was not certain that Rocky would be content to just fade away, but at age sixty-seven his political career seemed to be near its end.

'BELIEVE ME, AT MY AGE AND WITH MY PROBLEMS I DON'T EVEN THINK ABOUT IT.'

JERRY FEARING
Courtesy St. Paul Dispatch

CLYDE PETERSON
Courtesy Houston Chronicle

1975, The Register
and Tribune Syndicate

"Nothing like a little incentive to calm their yapping."

BOB TAYLOR
—By BOB TAYLOR   *Courtesy Dallas Times Herald*

"Sure nice of this fella to give us a lift—ain't it, Nelson?"

DOUG MARLETTE
Courtesy Charlotte Observer

"WHAT A SURPRISE—A VOLUNTEER!"

GEORGE FISHER
Courtesy N. Little Rock Times

Southern Strategy

JON KENNEDY
Courtesy Arkansas Democrat

'Boys will be boys'

Fifth Wheel

'RELAX, ROCKY, WE'RE BEHIND YOU 1,000%!'

ZSCHIESCHE KING FEATURES
BOB ZSCHIESCHE
©King Features

JIM PALMER
Courtesy Dallas News

The Energy Crisis

The Oil Producing and Exporting Countries (OPEC) cartel increased its annual income from petroleum in 1975 by another $10 billion. The oil cartel, which now realizes $110 billion annually, has boosted its prices 438 percent in two years. President Ford lamented the increase and chastised Congress for its inability to act.

The United States, nevertheless, seemed in a better position than other nations. America imports only about 38 percent of its total oil needs; Japan depends on imported oil for 100 percent of its need; West Germany and France buy roughly 95 percent of their fuel from oil-producing nations.

GEORGE FISHER
Courtesy N. Little Rock Times

"Let's help the Americans celebrate their bicentennial. Let's charge $17.76 per barrel."

SCOTT LONG
Courtesy Minneapolis Tribune

'We're Experiencing Some Difficulty With the Design'

CARL LARSEN
Courtesy Richmond Times-Dispatch

PIPELINE TO NOPLACE

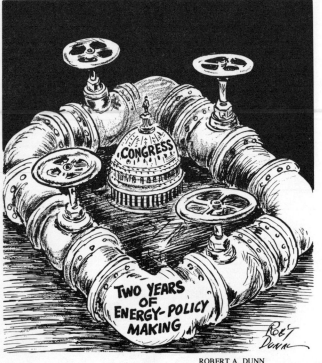

ROBERT A. DUNN
Courtesy Buffalo Courier-Express

ALI BABA AND THE 40 THIEVES -1975

JIM DOBBINS
Courtesy Boston Herald-American

KEN ALEXANDER
Courtesy San Francisco Examiner

TOM DARCY
Newsday
©Los Angeles Times Syndicate

Gums

DRAPER HILL
Courtesy The Commercial Appeal

TOM CURTIS
Courtesy Milwaukee Sentinel

"Save us, Fang!"

TOM INNES
Courtesy Calgary (Can.) Herald

". . . Could be he's privy to information
we're ignorant of."

GENE BASSET
Courtesy Scripps-Howard Newspapers

"That's it, Ali, do it just a shade or two browner!"

ROBERT GRAYSMITH
Courtesy San Francisco Chronicle

Smile

DON HESSE
Courtesy St. Louis Globe-Democrat

JOHN LANE
©NEA

Tune in next decade for the exciting conclusion

41

ED VALTMAN
©Trans-World News Service

" 'er, maybe you better return the rebate—it will just about cover my price increase on the gas"

JERRY BARNETT
Courtesy Indianapolis News

IT ONLY HURTS WHEN I DRIVE

EVENING JOURNAL
Wilmington, Del.

JACK JURDEN
Courtesy Wilmington Evening
Journal-News

EUGENE PAYNE
Courtesy WSOC-TV, Charlotte

"CAN WE SUPPLY FUEL? LEAVE EVERYTHING TO US AND WE'LL HAVE YOU SWIMMING IN IT"

OFFSHORE DRILLING

OIL POLITICS

GAS PRICES

FEDERAL ENERGY OFFICE

"RELEASE ME!"

EPA GAS MILEAGE TESTS

©1975 HERBLOCK

HERBLOCK
©Washington Post

ED FISCHER
Courtesy Omaha World-Herald

'NOW IT'S OFFICIAL — 130 MILES TO THE GALLON'

FRANK SPANGLER
Courtesy Montgomery (Ala.)
Advertiser

Wish Him Luck!

"BUY!"

TOM FLANNERY
Courtesy Baltimore Sun

GOING, GOING ~ ~ - - - - .

30¢ GAS

50¢ GAS

70¢ GAS

The Daily Oklahoman

JIM LANGE
The Daily Oklahoman
©The Oklahoma Publishing Co.

JON KENNEDY
Courtesy Arkansas Democrat

Quoth the raven, 'Nevermore'

LEONARD NORRIS
Courtesy Vancouver (Can.) Sun

"Multinational oil companies handing out millions in bribes around the world and what does he accept for doing business with them? A tumbler."

"IS THERE A HOUDINI IN THE HOUSE — OR SENATE ?"

HERC FICKLEN
Courtesy Dallas Morning News

JOHN CRAWFORD
Courtesy Alabama Journal

BERT WHITMAN
Courtesy Phoenix Gazette

"HOLD ON, MR. PRESIDENT. HERE COMES AN ADVISER WITH ANOTHER FUEL SAVING PLAN."

THE PROMISED LAND

The Middle East

The United States continued in its familiar role as middleman in the tinderbox of the Middle East throughout 1975.

On June 5 Egypt reopened the Suez Canal to international shipping, thus greatly increasing Cairo's stake in peace. Israel responded by reducing its forces on the Suez front and pulling missiles and artillery out of range of the Canal. In a significant move, Saudi Arabia's King Khalid declared his willingness to recognize the existence of Israel within its pre-1967 borders.

In late August, Henry Kissinger engineered an agreement under which Cairo renounced the use of force during the lifetime of the pact, and Israel withdrew its forces from strategic passes in the Sinai Desert and former Arab oil fields.

Washington agreed to commitments ranging from an outlay of billions of dollars in economic and military aid to both sides to a watchdog role. The stationing of American technicians in the Sinai buffer zone was hotly debated before Congress approved it.

Religious strife flared into civil war in Lebanon late in the year, threatening the tenuous Arab-Israeli peace.

"NOT THE AMERICAN PLANES, DUMMY! HOW MANY TIMES I GOTTA TELL YOU... NOT THE AMERICAN PLANES!"

ED GAMBLE
Courtesy Nashville Banner

"SPLENDID IDEA, HENRY...GET THE MAPS OUT AND WE'LL REASSESS OUR POSITION"

JOHN COLLINS
Courtesy Montreal (Can.) Gazette

RED SEA CROSSING

'Your move . . .'

ZSCHIESCHE
KING FEATURES
BOB ZSCHIESCHE
©King Features

V. ROSCHKOV
Courtesy Windsor Star

BILL ANDREWS
Courtesy New York Daily World

MIDEAST PEACE SIGN

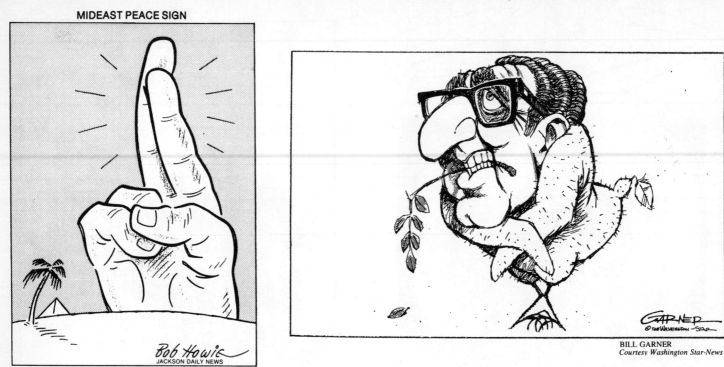

BOB HOWIE
Courtesy Jackson (Miss.) Daily News

BILL GARNER
Courtesy Washington Star-News

"HE'S NOT TO GET INVOLVED....MERELY OBSERVE!"

BOB PALMER
*Courtesy Springfield (Mo.)
   Leader-Press*

Soviet Grain Deal

Once again Russia turned to the United States for help in feeding its people, concluding an agreement that will lead to huge purchases of American grain during the next five years. Under the pact, the Soviets will buy at least six million metric tons of grain—about half wheat and half corn—annually for five years. A proviso allows the Russians to buy an additional two million tons a year, unless the United States has a poor crop.

But as for American purchases of Soviet oil, there was only a weak promise. Negotiations will continue regarding the possible sale of 200,000 barrels a day of Russian oil to the United States.

PAT OLIPHANT
Washington Star-News
©Los Angeles Times Syndicate
THE LOS ANGELES TIMES SYNDICATE
©1976 WASHINGTON STAR

'GET HIM TO TELL YOU THE ONE ABOUT THE BIG OIL AND WHEAT DEAL WITH RUSSIA!'

'EVER GET THAT FEELING OF BEING WATCHED?'

ROBERT A. DUNN
Courtesy Buffalo Courier-Express

RAY OSRIN
Courtesy Cleveland Plain Dealer

"I'M SORRY, BUT WE SEEM TO BE FRESH OUT"

WOMAN OVERBOARD!

JIM DOBBINS
Courtesy Boston Herald-American

EDDIE GERMANO
Courtesy Brockton Daily Enterprise

BETTER TAKE ANOTHER LOOK, SAM

KEVIN McVEY
Courtesy The Record, Hackensack, N. J.

JERRY BARNETT
Courtesy Indianapolis News

DAVID SIMPSON
Courtesy Tulsa Tribune

Crime

Statistics compiled by the FBI and released in 1975 showed that the United States experienced the most sizable jump in crime since the collection of such data began in 1930. Every type of serious crime increased—not only in the cities but in the suburbs as well.

Law enforcement officials complained of soft-hearted judges and short or nonexistent jail terms, contending that too often the guilty are merely put on probation. Figures indicate that repeat offenders are responsible for most major crimes.

Increased participation in violent crimes by women and by teenagers was also noted. According to a Chicago police official: "The largest group of lawbreakers in Chicago is between the ages of 15 and 20, and the next largest group is between 10 and 15."

Crime against business soared nationwide, with shoplifting, employee thievery, and hijacking accounting for the loss of some $20 billion a year.

CRAIG MACINTOSH
Courtesy Dayton Journal-Herald

'BOYS WILL BE BOYS, YOU GUYS RUN ALONG NOW, WE'LL TAKE CARE OF THE LADIES'

WAYNE STAYSKAL
Courtesy Chicago Tribune

BERT WHITMAN
Courtesy Phoenix Gazette

All in favor of reducing marijuana possession to the status of a minor traffic violation, say 'aye'

"HE'S NOT WITH ME....I THOUGHT HE WAS WITH YOU!"

DICK LOCHER
Courtesy Chicago Tribune

"Don't worry about it! Cruel and unusual punishment applies to us if we're caught! Not to our victims!"

WAYNE STAYSKAL
Courtesy Chicago Tribune

JACK LANIGAN
Courtesy New Bedford Standard-Times

" IT'S BLOOD !! "

When last seen . . .

VIC RUNTZ
Courtesy Bangor Daily News

Indira Gandhi

Indian Prime Minister Indira Gandhi, long a vocal critic of the United States and its foreign policy, almost overnight transformed the world's most populous democracy into a police state. Convicted of violating India's election laws, Mrs. Gandhi was banned from voting in parliament by court order. There were many calls for her resignation.

Then, on June 26, the fifty-seven-year-old daughter of Nehru, India's first prime minister, struck back, imposing a state of national emergency and ordering more than six hundred of her political enemies arrested. Many were dragged from their beds in the middle of the night.

Ironically, by thwarting civil disobedience, Mrs. Gandhi was attacking the primary weapon used by Mahatma Gandhi in his campaign to free India from British rule.

V. ROSCHKOV
Courtesy Windsor Star

BED OF NAILS

FRANK WILLIAMS
Courtesy Detroit Free Press

PAUL SZEP
Courtesy Boston Globe

"I am not a crook!"

BALDY
Courtesy Atlanta Constitution

"It distresses me so when people won't believe how deeply I am committed to democracy"

JOHN FISCHETTI
Courtesy Chicago Daily News

INDIRA'S PRESS

BLAINE
Courtesy The Spectator, Canada

ERIC SMITH
Courtesy Capital-Gazette (Md.) Newspapers

'IT WASN'T A STOP SIGN AFTER ALL!'

EUGENE CRAIG
Courtesy Columbus (O.) Dispatch

VIC CANTONE
©Editor and Publisher

MERLE TINGLEY
Courtesy London (Can.) Free Press

Detente

There was widespread feeling in Washington and across the country during the year that the policy of detente between the United States and Russia had been oversold by Secretary of State Henry Kissinger. Illusions that detente would solve all U.S.-Soviet conflicts virtually disappeared. In moves in Angola and elsewhere, Russia demonstrated anew that it is bent on expanding its influence at the expense of America wherever possible.

Contributing to Washington's second thoughts about detente were growing Communist strength in Portugal and Italy, Red victories in Indochina with Russian support, and the weakening of NATO's Mediterranean flank. And, in spite of the SALT agreements, detente seemed more and more a one-way street favoring Moscow.

Russia continues to increase its army, already twice the size of America's. The Soviets have more land-based missiles than the United States and are now challenging for the lead in sophisticated warheads.

JOHN FISCHETTI
Courtesy Chicago Daily News

'Not to worry. Is used only for coastal defense.!

ERIC SMITH
Courtesy Capital-Gazette (Md.) Newspapers

'What Happened to the Pandas We Sent You?'

JOHN STAMPONE
Courtesy Army Times

**'O beautiful for spacious skies
For amber waves of grain . . . '**

TONY AUTH
Philadelphia Enquirer
©Washington Post Writers' Group

ED GAMBLE
Courtesy Nashville Banner

BOB SULLIVAN
Courtesy Worcester (Mass.) Telegram

"Pleeze -- no more kickin' der sand in d'face!"

BILL GRAHAM
Courtesy Arkansas Gazette

"Cut . . . Cut! Fine Henry, now try it on TOP of the water, okay baby?"

"DOKTOR KISSINGER, I PRESUME?"

KARL HUBENTHAL
Courtesy Los Angeles
Herald-Examiner

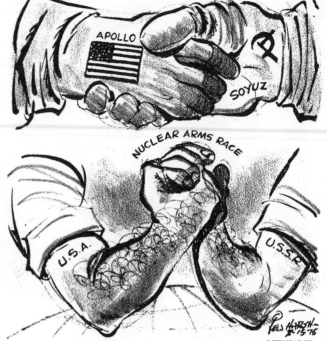

HANDS AND ARMS!

LEW HARSH
Courtesy Scranton Time

ED GAMBLE
Courtesy Nashville Banner

"EVERYTHING WENT FINE UNTIL THE AMERICANS BROKE OUR CONCENTRATION WITH THAT CONWAY TWITTY RECORDING!"

RATIFICATION OF BETRAYAL

1945
YALTA
AGREEMENT

HELSINKI
CONFIRMATION
1975

KARL HUBENTHAL
*Courtesy Los Angeles
Herald-Examiner*

U.S. NAVY

USSR Sea Power

EVENING JOURNAL
Wilmington, Del.

JANE'S FIGHTING SHIPS

JACK JURDEN
Courtesy Wilmington Evening Journal-News

JERRY FEARING
Courtesy St. Paul Dispatch

TOM CURTIS
Courtesy Milwaukee Sentinel

US FOREIGN POLICY

"At least we've still got detente, eh, Mr. Brezhnev?"

JIM KNUDSEN
Courtesy San Diego Union

RUSSIAN OCCUPATION

EASTERN EUROPE

'IT'S GOING TO BE PARKED HERE PERMANENTLY'

While Uncle Builds the Road

U.S.

DETENTE

COMMUNIZE THE WORLD

PAP DEAN 5-25-75
THE SHREVEPORT TIMES
PAP DEAN
Courtesy Shreveport Times

EUROPEAN SECURITY CONFERENCE

HELSINKI

MUTUAL TRUST · INVIOLABILITY · NON-INTERFERENCE · NON-INTERFERENCE · MUTUAL TRUST · INVIOLABILITY

'DO YOU THINK HE'D MIND IF WE TOOK THESE OFF WHEN WE GET AROUND THE CORNER?'

AWAKE!!

ALEXANDER SOLZHENITSYN

THE SOVIET THREAT

"COMFORTABLE?"

"OH YES, QUITE COMFORTABLE"

détente

HELSINKI LOVE SEAT

'Let's have another one'

Educational Problems

Throughout the United States in 1975 a heated debated raged between parents and educators over who should decide what and how school children are to be taught. A major conflict centered on school textbooks, as in Kanawka County, West Virginia, where protests were most violent. There, as elsewhere, parents charged that many required textbooks were obscene, anti-American, or anti-Christian.

In other communities, officials and parent groups sought measures to quell growing disorders that frequently disrupted classrooms and made schoolgrounds unsafe. At many schools teachers reported they actually feared for their lives.

In Boston and Louisville, opposition to court-ordered busing erupted into violence when schools opened in September. Rallies were held in both cities, and angry parents marched, to no avail. In Boston's Southie area, large numbers of white parents enrolled their children in four all-white academies. Other pupils simply sat out much of the term.

Nationwide studies conducted in 1975 indicated a serious lessening of student achievement. Average test scores of 10.5 million youngsters dropped two percent in three years, and a dramatic drop in student writing skills threatened to become a national scandal.

"Steady there Miss Figsby...we haven't achieved the ideal pupil-teacher ratio. You just forgot it's Saturday."

LEONARD NORRIS
Courtesy Vancouver (Can.) Sun

"ELEPHANT? WHAT ELEPHANT?"

"I'll bet it's the same mob of crazies who bombed us who are now stoning those Black schoolkids in Boston!"

'.. AND HERE WE KEEP THE SOCIOLOGISTS WHO RECOMMENDED FORCED BUSING IN THE FIRST PLACE!"

DWANE POWELL
Courtesy Cincinnati Enquirer

'REASONABLE FORCE, MISS GRUNDY, REASONABLE FORCE...'

JOHN FISCHETTI
Courtesy Chicago Daily News

"MY KID'S A PUPIL IN YOUR CLASS AND HE WANTS TO KNOW WHAT THE SIGN SAYS"

'DON'T YOU HEAR ME? – I SAID FULL SPEED AHEAD'

DON HESSE
Courtesy St. Louis Globe-Democrat

CHARLES BROOKS
Courtesy Birmingham (Ala.) News

Speaking of Enclaves

DRAPER HILL
Courtesy The Commercial Appeal

GUERNSEY LEPELLEY
Courtesy Christian Science Monitor

'Er . . . no . . . I don't think forced busing of teachers is legal . . .'

73

PAUL SZEP
Courtesy Boston Globe

"Don't just stand there . . . . . do something!"

PART OF MY BACK T'SCHOOL SUPPLIES

CHESTER COMMODORE
Courtesy Chicago Daily Defender

CRAIG MACINTOSH
Courtesy Dayton Journal-Herald

'AS PART OF OUR SERIES ON THE TRI-CENTENNIAL, WE HAVE RE-CREATED A STREET SCENE FROM BOSTON, 1975'

JACK GOLD
Courtesy Kentucky Post

74

CIA—FBI

A storm of controversy swirled around the Central Intelligence Agency and the Federal Bureau of Investigation during the year. Following an intensive investigation, the Rockefeller Commission found evidence of illegal domestic spying by the CIA, as well as involvement in assassination plots against foreign leaders. Senator Frank Church of Idaho headed a Senate committee probing deeper into many of these charges.

On November 20, in an unprecedented act, the Senate Select Committee on Intelligence released a 346-page report of previously secret details concerning American intelligence operations. Many citizens felt that the action was unnecessary and damaging to the U.S. intelligence effort.

Inside Job

TOM ENGELHARDT
Courtesy St. Louis Post-Dispatch

Late in the year the Senate Select Committee, after another lengthy investigation, declared that the FBI had been vulnerable to "political abuse" and that it had happened under every President from Franklin D. Roosevelt to Richard Nixon. Citing the late director, J. Edgar Hoover, as the chief culprit, the committee reported that the FBI had been willing to carry out illegal presidential requests over the years.

ROB LAWLOR
Courtesy Philadelphia Daily News

JIM KNUDSEN
Courtesy San Diego Union

"IF THEY PUT US IN A GOLDFISH BOWL, WHO'LL KEEP AN EYE ON THE SHARKS?"

DICK WALLMEYER
Long Beach Press-Telegram
©Register and Tribune Syndicate

This Is Your FBI

DENNIS RENAULT
©McClatchy Newspapers

BOB SULLIVAN
Courtesy Worcester Telegram

TOM DARCY
Newsday
©Los Angeles Times Syndicate

ART BIMROSE
Courtesy Portland Oregonian

THE NEW FALL SEASON

CAUGHT IN THE HEN HOUSE

ROBERT GRAYSMITH
Courtesy San Francisco Chronicle

THE PROTESTERS MARCH

ALL CONGRESS MUST KNOW WHAT CIA IS DOING!

NO SECRETS DOWN WITH THE CIA

WHO NEEDS THE CIA?

RUSSIA'S SPY NETWORK

BROOKS THE BIRMINGHAM NEWS

CHARLES BROOKS
Courtesy Birmingham (Ala.) News

DICK WRIGHT
Courtesy San Diego Union

WRIGHT COPLEY NEWSPAPERS

CIA

U.S. MAIL

CRAWFORD ADVERTISER-JOURNAL
JOHN CRAWFORD
Courtesy Alabama Journal

PRES. FO

LIBERTY

'CIA IN THE WHITE HOUSE ? .... ABSOLUTELY RIDICULOUS.'

Omaha World-Herald
The Newspaper of the Midlands

Federal Bureau
of Investigation
Washington, D.C.

Dear FBI,

Do you have a
file on me?

Sincerely,
Ed Fischer
Omaha, Nebrask

Ed Fischer
Omaha, Nebraska

Dear Ed:

We do now.

Sincerely,
FB Eye
Your FBI

ED FISCHER
Courtesy Omaha World-Herald

DO YOU THINK THEY WILL CALL THE CIA UP ON THE CARPET?

CIA ABUSES

CHARLES DANIEL
Courtesy Knoxville Journal

GUERNSEY LEPELLEY
Courtesy Christian Science Monitor

CONGRESS INVESTIGATING COMMITTEE

CIA SKULDUGGERY

"If it walks around, there ought to be somebody in there"

80

OLLIE HARRINGTON
Courtesy New York Daily World

ART HENRIKSON
Courtesy Des Plaines (Ill.) Herald

We've been looking for a guy
with his skills — 26 years burglarizing for the FBI!

MIKE KEEFE
Courtesy Denver Post

'AH . . . ANOTHER SPECIAL DELIVERY!'

JOHN PIEROTTI
Courtesy New York Post

FRANK TYGER
Courtesy Trenton Times

"There are times when I think it deserves to be called our Central Unintelligent Agency."

DAVID SEAVEY
©National Observer

Canadian Affairs

Canadian nationalism, aimed at decreasing American influence, gained official government sanction in 1975. New official policies were designed to reduce U.S. control over business and industry in Canada, and efforts were made to reduce American influence through movies, books, magazines, television, sports, and art. "Yankee Go Home" signs were directed at American tourists in Ottawa.

On October 21 postal workers began the largest postal strike in Canada's history. Canadians resorted to private couriers, delivery by hand, and even crossing the border to mail letters and packages in the United States. Striking workers received a 38 percent pay hike before the strike was settled in late December.

GRAHAM PILSWORTH
Courtesy Toronto Star

PETER KUCH
Courtesy Winnipeg Free Press

MERLE TINGLEY
Courtesy London (Can.) Free Press

ROY CARLESS
Courtesy Steel Labor U.S.W.A., Canada

JOHN COLLINS
Courtesy Montreal (Can.) Gazette

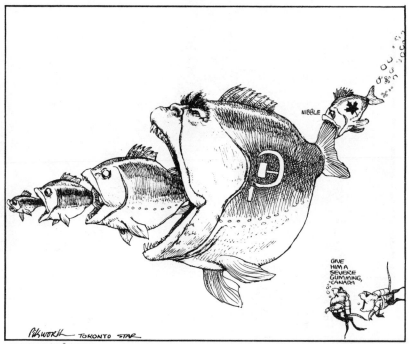

GRAHAM PILSWORTH
Courtesy Toronto Star

Foreign Affairs

Visits by President Ford to China and East European Communist countries highlighted American overtures on the international scene in 1975. His five-day visit for summit talks with Chinese leaders in December left many Americans wondering if the trip was really worthwhile. The U.S.-Peking relationship is a unique one. The two countries are not allies, but each seeks to do business with the other—for different reasons. Russia is involved in both reasons. The United States hopes to use China to keep detente with Russia on an even keel, while Peking sees this country as a balancing wheel in Chinese relations with the Soviet Union, a feared enemy.

Ford's August meeting in Helsinki with Leonid Brezhnev was viewed by many observers as an overwhelming Russian triumph. Brezhnev gained a prize he had sought for years—a substitute treaty that lends legitimacy to the grab of Eastern Europe by the U.S.S.R. after World War II.

Fidel Castro made it known during the year that Cuba would welcome renewed ties with the United States, but Cuban intervention in the Angola conflict left the Ford administration cool toward the idea.

DRAPER HILL
Courtesy The Commercial Appeal

The Reception of the Diplomatique & his Suite at the Court of Peking.

FOREIGN AFFAIRS

Senator George McGovern was one of several congressional figures to visit Havana during the year.

Japanese Emperor Hirohito made a celebrated visit to Washington as Ford's guest, the first such visit by a Japanese monarch.

Representatives of the six most powerful industrial nations in the Western World met in Paris in November to forge a framework of unity in an effort to achieve economic recovery. It was obvious, however, that they still held many key differences, particularly in energy policies.

TOM CURTIS
Courtesy Milwaukee Sentinel

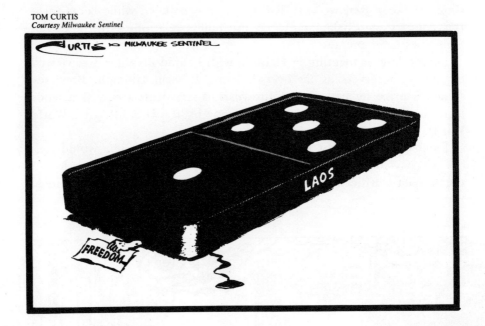

... ANOTHER RED EPITAPH ...

VERN THOMPSON
Courtesy Lawton (Okla.) Constitution

HY ROSEN
Courtesy Albany Times-Union

"...AND HE SAYS TELL GEORGE NOT TO OVERDO IT!"

'I Feel So Very Much at Home'

ELDON PLETCHER
*Courtesy New Orleans
Times-Picayune*

JACK McLEOD
Courtesy Buffalo Evening News

V-J PLUS THIRTY YEARS

" TORA! TORA! TORA! "

BOB ENGLEHART
Courtesy Dayton Journal Herald

87

ANDY DONATO
Courtesy Toronto Sun

HY ROSEN
Courtesy Albany Times-Union

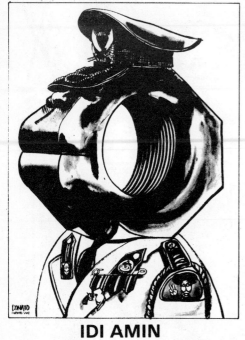

IDI AMIN

"HOW DO YOU MAKE EGG FOO KISSINGER? VERY DELICATELY!"

BLAINE
Courtesy The Spectator, Canada

The End in Vietnam

After a seemingly endless struggle that threatened to tear America apart, the war in Vietnam finally came to an end in April, 1975. Nearly 57,000 lives were lost and $150 billion spent in America's longest war.

It was a bitter defeat for a nation that had never lost a war. The world witnessed in wonder the spectacle of the last Americans in Vietnam scrambling aboard helicopters to escape as Communist troops swarmed into Saigon. For many, it remains the greatest humiliation the United States has ever endured; the military forces of the strongest and

THE LIGHT AT THE END OF THE TUNNEL

KARL HUBENTHAL
*Courtesy Los Angeles
Herald-Examiner*

richest nation in the history of the world had been driven out by a small, impoverished, third-rate country that has barely moved into the industrialized twentieth century.

Some 100,000 South Vietnamese refugees were able to reach safety in the United States, while thousands of others were reportedly killed after the takeover because of their past association with Americans.

MIKE PETERS
Courtesy Dayton Daily News

Peace at Last

CARL LARSEN
Courtesy Richmond Times-Dispatch

'WHY BOTHER, HE'S GONNA DIE ANYWAY!'

JIM PALMER
Courtesy Dallas News

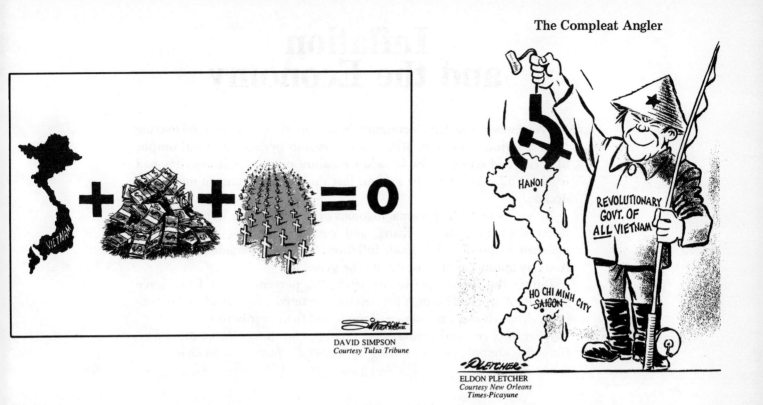

DAVID SIMPSON
Courtesy Tulsa Tribune

ELDON PLETCHER
Courtesy New Orleans
Times-Picayune

'WE'RE PASSING AROUND A PETITION TO KEEP THOSE VIETNAM FOREIGNERS OUT OF OUR COMMUNITY'

SANDY CAMPBELL
Courtesy The Tennessean

Inflation
and the Economy

By November the U.S. economy began to show signs of recovering from a serious recession. Within a five-month period, the total output of goods and services—the broadest measure of economic activity—had regained 37 percent of the ground lost during the seventeen months of decline.

By year's end, the personal incomes of many citizens were increasing faster than the cost of living, and consumer buying power almost matched its prerecession level. Inflation, however, remained a problem, rising by about 7.6 percent during the year.

During the fourth quarter of 1975, 8.3 percent of the labor force was out of work. This high percentage remained a matter of major concern, although more people were employed than ever before.

After two years of conservative buying, consumers broke loose on a Christmas shopping spree, setting sales records from coast to coast.

BALDY
Courtesy Atlanta Constitution

"...I DON'T KNOW WHEN BUT I WON YOU A HELLUVA CONTRACT IF IT DOES!"

JOHN CHASE
Louisiana Newspapers

ED VALTMAN
©Trans-World News Service

'FOR A MOMENT I THOUGHT I SAW THE LIGHT AT THE END OF THE TUNNEL'

BOB BECKETT
Courtesy WCAU-TV, Philadelphia

LOU ERICKSON
Courtesy Atlanta Journal

MIKE KEEFE
Courtesy Denver Post

JOHN FISCHETTI
Courtesy Chicago Daily News

"FOLLOW ANY CAR! QUICK!"

THE FRONT VIEW IS FINE —

US LIVING HABITS

"I'm glad I majored in economics. I now have a clearer understanding of why there's no job waiting for me out there.

CAN YOU DANCE?

FRYING PAN OR FIRE

"DO YOU BELIEVE WE'RE IN A DEPRESSION, A RECESSION, OR JUST EXPERIENCING SEVERE INFLATION?"

"No, this isn't the line for 'Godfather II,' it's Unemployment '75"

JIM BERRY
©NEA

BOB BECKETT
Courtesy WCAU-TV, Philadelphia

© 1975 by NEA, Inc.

"The poor consumer! He never used to have so many troubles until all these consumer advocates came on to the scene!"

RAY OSRIN
Courtesy Cleveland Plain Dealer

"THIS IS YOUR CAPTAIN SPEAKING...WE JUST WANT TO REASSURE YOU THAT YOU ARE EXPERIENCING A PERFECTLY NORMAL BOTTOMING OUT..."

C. F. MORSE
©Hearst Newspapers

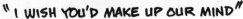

U.S. ECONOMY

TAX REBATE

CONGRESS

"I WISH YOU'D MAKE UP OUR MIND"

INFLATION

RECESSION

BYRON HUMPHREY
Courtesy New Orleans States-Item

THE ONLY PLACE BLACKS BUILD UP SENIORITY

UNEMPLOYMENT LINE

CHESTER COMMODORE
Courtesy Chicago Daily Defender

CORPORATE INDUSTRIAL DISEASE CEMETERY

OUR GATES ARE ALWAYS OPEN

DIED IN THE NAME OF PRODUCTIVITY

ROY CARLESS
Courtesy Steel Labor U.S.W.A.,
Canada

DEPT. OF SANITATION

THE REALLY DEGRADING PART IS: THERE ARE SOME SCHOOL TEACHERS MAKE MORE THAN WE DO!

TRULY A SHAME

98

JACK GOLD
Courtesy Kentucky Post

DICK LOCHER
Courtesy Chicago Tribune

"Golly, what a beautiful ship...! What makes it go?"

DENNIS RENAULT
©McClatchy Newspapers

CHARLES BISSELL
Courtesy Nashville Tennessean

"Someday, son, this will all be yours. And your son's. And your son's son's. And your son's son's son's. And his son's. And his son's son's . . ."

"Poor old beast of burden! . . . He's carrying the building materials for the Democratic Platform."

ETTA HULME
Courtesy Ft. Worth Star-Telegram

"BY GEORGE, MEANY—YOUR BLOOD PRESSURE IS RELATED DIRECTLY TO THE WHOLESALE PRICE INDEX"

EUGENE PAYNE
Courtesy WSOC-TV, Charlotte

Inflation hasn't slowed travel

HANDWRITING ON THE WALL.

ART POINIER
Courtesy Detroit News

CLYDE PETERSON
Courtesy Houston Chronicle

"Hey, outa the way! Ya some kinda scab?!"

FRANK INTERLANDI
©Los Angeles Times Syndicate

"Looks rosy!"

Welfare

Controversy continued to envelop the nation's burgeoning welfare program, which in 1975 saw some 18 million Americans receiving food stamps and 15 million others being provided some form of public assistance. During the past decade, welfare spending jumped 32 percent—from less than one-third of the federal budget to some 55 percent.

President Ford seemed determined to hold down welfare spending in 1976 and announced plans to tighten eligibility requirements, police them more closely, and press recipients to look for work. An overhaul of the vast Department of Health, Education and Welfare seemed in order, and the new HEW secretary, F. David Mathews, began work on a reorganizational plan.

It was disclosed that food stamps are provided in some cases to families with incomes of $12,000 a year. Schoolteachers, policemen, military families, and retirees are receiving food stamp assistance from Uncle Sam.

DENNIS RENAULT
©McClatchy Newspapers

"Dear President Ford: I am an orphan and my life is in danger. Fly me to freedom."

ART HENRIKSON
Courtesy Des Plaines (Ill.) Herald

STATE U.

P

POOR GUY!

RELATIVELY SPEAKING, THAT IS

They're trying to tighten up the food stamp program. I may have to sell my Cadillac!

Could It Be He's Out of Control?

AGRICULTURE DEPT.

FOOD STAMP PROGRAM

PAP DEAN
Courtesy Shreveport Times

'NO, I THINK THAT'S YOUR BALL!'

STATES

WELFARE

EUGENE CRAIG
Courtesy Columbus (O.) Dispatch

WELFARE

CITIES

BUDGET WOES

AL LIEDERMAN
Courtesy Long Island Press

103

Assassinations

Assassination remained a very real threat for American leaders as President Ford survived two attempts on his life within a seventeen-day period. Both of the alleged would-be assassins were women.

Lynette Fromme, a follower of convicted mass-murderer Charles Manson, was charged with attempting to shoot Ford with a pistol at point-blank range on September 5 in Sacramento, California. Apparently the gun jammed and did not fire. She was convicted in December of attempted assassination of the President, an unprecedented conviction.

Less than three weeks later, in San Francisco, Sara Jane Moore allegedly fired at Ford from across the street as he emerged from a building, but the shot missed him. A bystander reportedly hit her arm and deflected the shot.

Public officials and private citizens as well called upon President Ford to curtail his travels and avoid mingling with crowds. A Gallup Poll showed that 45 percent of the public believed that "the risk is too great" for the President to move among crowds shaking hands.

GENE BASSET
Courtesy Scripps-Howard Newspapers

"LOOK, FELLERS, IF I DON'T WORRY, WHY SHOULD YOU?"

TOM ENGELHARDT
Courtesy St. Louis Post-Dispatch

ENGELHARDT

The American Madness

JOHN RIEDELL
Courtesy Peoria Journal

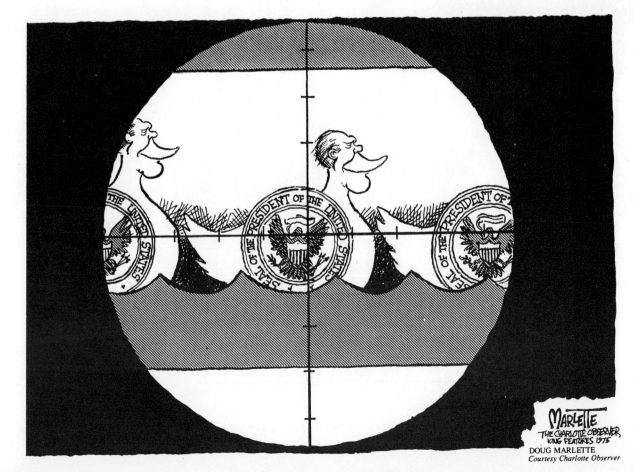

DOUG MARLETTE
Courtesy Charlotte Observer

ART POINIER
Courtesy Detroit News

'PRESSING THE FLESH'

SCOTT LONG
Courtesy Minneapolis Tribune

LEW HARSH
Courtesy Scranton Times

". . . AND IF YOU PLAN TO RUN FOR PUBLIC OFFICE —
IT COMES WITH A BULLET-PROOF VEST!"

Robert E. Lee, Citizen

Robert E. Lee posthumously regained his American citizenship in 1975 as a result of congressional action. General Lee was stripped of his citizenship because of his service as commanding general of the Confederate Army during the Civil War.

After the peace was signed at Appomattox in 1865, Lee sought a pardon in order to regain his citizenship. He swore out the required oath of allegiance to the United States, but the document apparently was misplaced and therefore never acted upon.

JEFF MACNELLY
Richmond News Leader
©Chicago Tribune—New York
News Syndicate

"I HEARD THE RED TAPE WAS BAD, BUT THIS IS RIDICULOUS...."

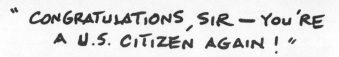

"CONGRATULATIONS, SIR — YOU'RE A U.S. CITIZEN AGAIN!"

ED ASHLEY
Courtesy Toledo Blade

GARRY APGAR
Courtesy Roanoke Times and World-News

New York City

New York City, on the brink of bankruptcy, was rescued from default by President Ford and the Congress with a pledge in December of federal loans and a multi-billion-dollar financing package backed by the state of New York. The financial plan to save the city's economy provides that:

The city will increase taxes some $200 million, in addition to $330 million in new taxes voted in September;

Require increased contributions to the city's pension plans by municipal workers; and

An additional spending cut of $524 million during the next two years.

Some $600 million already had been cut from the city's budget and more than 35,000 jobs eliminated as Mayor Abraham Beame sought to cope with the financial collapse.

The federal government will lend up to $2.3 billion a year to New York State to help provide for the city's short-term cash needs through mid-1978. The loans are to be repaid by the end of each fiscal year.

TONY AUTH
Philadelphia Enquirer
©Washington Post Writers' Group

JAMES MORGAN
Courtesy Spartanburg Herald-Journal

JERRY ROBINSON
©Chicago Tribune-N.Y. News Syndicate

GENE BASSET
Courtesy Scripps-Howard Newspapers

NOT TOO LOUD, PLEASE

DOUG SNEYD
Courtesy Toronto Star

WARREN KING
Courtesy N.Y. Daily News

*"If the meek really shall inherit the earth, Father, it'd
be just my luck to wind up with New York."*

"NEW YORK CITY IS STILL THE BIG APPLE" — N.Y. CITY MAYOR, ABE BEAME —

VERN THOMPSON
Courtesy Lawton (Okla.) Constitution

'SO HE'S GOING TO CRASH — THAT'S HIS PROBLEM'

JERRY FEARING
Courtesy St. Paul Dispatch

ATSEFF SYRACUSE HERALD-JOURNAL

TIMOTHY ATSEFF
Courtesy Syracuse Herald-Journal

JERRY ROBINSON
©Chicago Tribune-N.Y. News Syndicate

ELDON PLETCHER
Courtesy New Orleans
Times-Picayune

JIM IVEY
Orlando Sentinel Star
©Rothco Cartoons, Inc.

JACK McLEOD
Courtesy Buffalo Evening News

'IF YOU DROWN, HAVE YOUR BANKER GIVE ME A CALL'

113

"YEAR OF THE LOCUST"

ART POINIER
Courtesy Detroit News

JIM DOBBINS
Courtesy Boston Herald-American

ROBERT GRAYSMITH
Courtesy San Francisco Chronicle

"Lucky break for us — the leak is in THEIR end of the boat"

"YOU SHOULD HAVE BEEN HERE IN THE OLD DAYS, BEFORE THE BUDGET CUTBACKS,,,,, THERE WERE COPS AND FIRE ENGINES AND PLANES BUZZING AROUND,,,,"

PAT OLIPHANT
Washington Star-News
©Los Angeles Times Syndicate

'CLASS! THAT'S ONE THING THEY CAN'T TAKE AWAY FROM US NEW YORKERS — OUR CLASS!'

DOUG MARLETTE
Courtesy Charlotte Observer

"I DON'T WANNA GET INVOLVED!"

"WHILE WE'RE WAITING FOR HELP, ANYBODY CARE TO BAIL?"

TRAVELING SALESMAN

IF IT CAN HAPPEN TO A BIG GUY LIKE HIM---

"THE DIFFERENCE BETWEEN WE AND THEE...IS _ YOU OWN THE PRINTING PRESS!"

Patty Hearst

After a 19-month chase, the FBI finally captured heiress Patty Hearst in late September to conclude one of the most bizarre criminal escapades in American history. Miss Hearst had been kidnapped by a group calling themselves the Symbionese Liberation Army. A few weeks later, in tape recordings sent to various news media, she renounced her family and declared she was joining ranks with her captors as an urban guerrilla fighter, and assumed the name Tania.

Captured with Patty was her close friend, Wendy Yoshimura. An hour earlier the FBI had arrested two other members of the now-decimated SLA—William Harris and his wife, Emily.

ROB LAWLOR
Courtesy Philadelphia Daily News

"That's right, completely innocent ... now as for those seven dwarfs ... !"

"You must believe that I'm a sweet, innocent, brainwashed victim . . . or else Tania will be forced to . . . ."

"STREETS OF SAN FRANCISCO"

Congressional Inaction

In Congress, 1975 was a year of politics. Two years after the Arab oil embargo, Congress still had not come up with a workable energy policy. Consumer bills, once considered certain of passage, had rough going. No-fault automobile insurance and a consumer-advocate agency got nowhere.

Caught up in politics, too, were a national health insurance system, welfare reform, tax reform, and forced busing of schoolchildren.

For millions of Americans, the big question became: When will Congress do something about the pressing problems of the day? At

HUGH HAYNIE
Louisville Courier-Journal
©Los Angeles Times Syndicate

"We have met the enemy . . . and he is us."

CONGRESSIONAL INACTION

year's end, however, it appeared that politics would dominate public policy again in 1976.

Polls repeatedly showed a serious decline in public esteem for Congress. In matters of defense, particularly, the Congress seemed either unable or unwilling to act.

BILL GARNER
Courtesy Washington Star-News

BRICKMAN
©Washington Star Syndicate
and King Features

PINOCCHIO

DON HESSE
Courtesy St. Louis Globe-Democrat

ART HENRIKSON
Courtesy Des Plaines (Ill.) Herald

Thank-you note

BILL ANDREWS
Courtesy New York Daily World

CONGRESS IN ACTION

JIM BERRY
©NEA

"I think I'll take the day off. I'm not feeling responsive to the people!"

A study in motion

AN INCH PER YEAR—

CONGRESS

IN PURSUIT OF SOLUTIONS FOR NATIONAL PROBLEMS

SPEED OF LIGHT

CONGRESS

ZAP

SALARY INCREASE FOR HIMSELF

REG MANNING
Courtesy Arizona Republic

CONGRESS

JER

DAVID SIMPSON
Courtesy Tulsa Tribune

"Sometimes we mule skinners have to give a little ground."

ETTA HULME
Courtesy Ft. Worth Star-Telegram

MIKE KEEFE
Courtesy Denver Post

'IS THIS YOUR STAMP OF APPROVAL?'

MERLE CUNNINGTON
Courtesy Valley News (Calif.)

LOOSE IN THE CHINA SHOP

"OH SAY CAN YOU SEE....."

ART WOOD
*Courtesy U. S. Independent
Telephone Assn.*

TOM CURTIS
Courtesy Milwaukee Sentinel

"We're off to a great start, Igor!"

LEW HARSH
Courtesy Scranton Times

"WHO SAYS THE 94ᵗʰ IS A DO-NOTHIN' CONGRESS?"

JOHN TREVER
Courtesy Sentinel Newspapers, Denver

"Hi! My name's Wanda Klutzsmith and here's my idea for public transportation . . ."

Gun Control

Because of the two attempts to shoot President Ford, debate was renewed in Congress over gun control. Both houses of Congress were deluged with gun legislation—130 such bills were offered in the House alone.

Opinion, of course, was sharply divided over the need for more firearms laws and their effect on crime. Equally vocal citizens, including members of the National Rifle Association, expressed concern for the rights of law-abiding gun owners. Advocates for stricter gun laws point to the fact that handguns were used in 10,323 murders in 1973, more than half of all reported that year. They also note that firearms were used in nearly two-thirds of the robberies in the same year.

Opponents of tighter control argue that "guns don't kill—people do," and that although law-abiding citizens will give up their guns, the criminals will certainly hold on to theirs.

WAYNE STAYSKAL
Courtesy Chicago Tribune

'DOES THIS MEAN WE'RE FINALLY CIVILIZED?'

ACME
BULLETPROOF
VEST INC.

GUNS
DON'T KILL-
PEOPLE
DO!

ROB LAWLOR
Courtesy Philadelphia Daily News

FRANK SPANGLER
*Courtesy Montgomery (Ala.)
Advertiser*

FIREARM AVAILABILITY

FORD

1975

1865   1881
    1901   1963

Still At It

DICK LOCHER
Courtesy Chicago Tribune

GUN
LOBBY

130

Betty Ford

The nation's First Lady, Betty Ford, found herself embroiled in a national controversy because of her outspoken comments on premarital sex and drugs. Although some viewed her remarks as admirable, candid, and refreshing, others considered them as a horrendous example of foot-in-mouth disease.

When interviewed by Morley Safer on CBS-TV's "60 Minutes" in August, Mrs. Ford said she assumed her four children had sampled marijuana and that she probably would have tried it herself had it been available when she was young. In response to Safer's question about her reaction should her eighteen-year-old daughter, Susan, become involved

PAUL CONRAD
Los Angeles Times
©Los Angeles Times Syndicate

in a premarital affair, the First Lady replied: "Well, I wouldn't be surprised. I think she's a perfectly normal human being like all young girls. If she wanted to continue, I would certainly counsel and advise her on the subject. . . . She's pretty young to start affairs, but she's a big girl."

Later the First Family's son Jack declared publicly that he had smoked pot and found it no more harmful than beer or wine.

At year's end, the jury was still out on whether such candor had helped or hurt the President's bid in the upcoming presidential election.

DON HESSE
Courtesy St. Louis Globe-Democrat

"I'm trying to find out what Betty meant so I can explain it to the press."

still life®

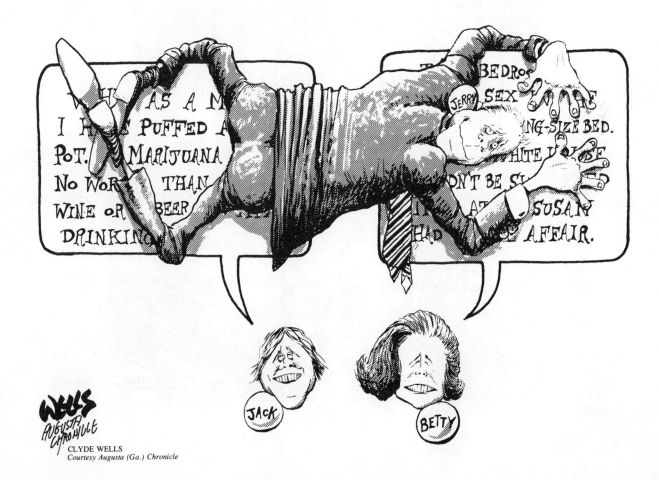

PILLOW TALK

JERRY BARNETT
Courtesy Indianapolis News

"Congratulations m'boy—It's not every newsman who can come up with a question Betty Ford won't answer."

DRAPER HILL
Courtesy The Commercial Appeal

'You May Have to Go, Rocky. I Can't Have
Two Liberal Running Mates'

TOM HAYGOOD
Courtesy San Antonio Light

Malpractice Insurance

The cost of physicians' malpractice insurance soared in 1975, dramatically increasing their fees for health care and sending many of them out on strike. Citing the rising number of malpractice suits against doctors, many old-line companies ceased writing malpractice insurance altogether.

There is no doubt that malpractice suits against doctors are increasing so rapidly and becoming so costly that they are altering the practice of medicine throughout the United States. During the past five years malpractice suits have more than doubled—they now total some eighteen million to twenty million claims a year—and the size of the claims and awards is going through the roof. It is not uncommon for sympathetic juries to award damages totaling hundreds of thousands of dollars.

In 1969, only 4 percent of all doctors faced malpractice suits. But in 1974, 10 percent faced pending suits, and during 1975 the percentage rose even higher. Experts have warned that the malpractice malady could destroy effective medical care.

DAVID SIMPSON
Courtesy Tulsa Tribune

"I can't finish him, Igor...I couldn't afford malpractice insurance this year!"

"But Consider the Alternatives!"

BILL CRAWFORD
©NEA

"You're gonna have to cut out my what?!"

BOB BECKETT '75
Courtesy WCAU-TV, Philadelphia

TOM DARCY
Newsday
©Los Angeles Times Syndicate

S. C. RAWLS
Courtesy Palm Beach Post

'DR. FRANKENSTEIN... YOUR MONSTER IS
SUEING YOU FOR MALPRACTICE'

"DR. FRANKENSTEIN, I'M SUING YOU
FOR MALPRACTICE."

U.N. and World Problems

Once again the United Nations found its stature diminished throughout most of the world by its actions and, in some cases, by its inaction. On November 10 the General Assembly voted seventy-two to thirty-five, with thirty-two abstentions, that Zionism is "a form of racism and racial discrimination." Offered by the militant Arab states, the resolution was supported heavily by Communist and Third World nations.

POLLUTION

CHARLES WERNER
Courtesy Indianapolis Star

The vote led some of the organization's staunchest defenders to wonder if the UN has outlived its usefulness.

Earlier, the dictator of Uganda, Idi Amin, addressed the UN on behalf of the forty-six-member Organization of African Unity. He called for the expulsion of Israel from the UN and for "the extinction of Israel as a State." Repeatedly throughout the year Third World leaders used the UN General Assembly to gang up on the United States, labeling America "imperialistic, aggressive, racist, and the exploiter of poor nations."

U.S. Ambassador to the United Nations Daniel O. Moynihan responded by calling Amin "a racist murderer" and contended that most African states had ended up as "enemies of freedom as we have tried to preserve it."

PAT OLIPHANT
Washington Star-News
©Los Angeles Times Syndicate

THE CANNIBALS

NO PLACE FOR WEAK LINKS

BILL CRAWFORD
©NEA

CARL E. BIEBER
Courtesy N. Platte (Neb.) Telegraph

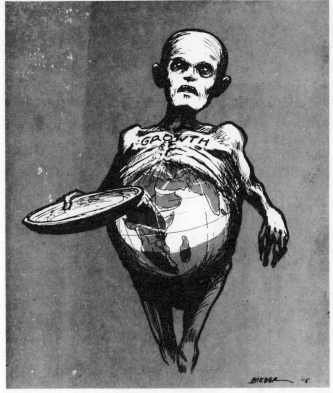

THE BELLY-ACHE

BOB PALMER
*Courtesy Springfield (Mo.)
Leader-Press*

JOHN PIEROTTI
Courtesy New York Post

HUGH HAYNIE
Louisville Courier-Journal
©Los Angeles Times Syndicate

The night the inmates took
over the asylum

BILL MAULDIN
©Chicago Sun-Times

"It's packed with midgets, all leaning the same
way."

UNITED NATIONS . . . SORT OF

AL LIEDERMAN
Courtesy Long Island Press

REMEMBER WHAT HAPPENED TO GULLIVER!

"YOU'D BETTER CURB YOUR PET"

MILT MORRIS
©The Associated Press

C. F. MORSE
©Hearst Newspapers

THE TROJAN STORK

KEN ALEXANDER
Courtesy San Francisco Examiner

European Instability

Europe was rocked by a series of events during 1975 that left many of its nations reeling and aroused grave concern for their future. Great Britain, of course, remained politically ill throughout the year, perhaps the sickest nation in the Western Alliance. Inflation rose by 25 percent, and the Gross National Product fell to less than half that of Germany and only slightly ahead of Italy's. Although Italy made attempts to combat a similar rate of inflation, unemployment rose to over one million. In June elections, Italian Communists achieved substantial victories and increased the prospect of a left-of-center government.

Spain's Generalissimo Francisco Franco died at the age of eighty-two, elevating Juan Carlos de Borbon to the throne and touching off widespread unrest and demands for dramatic political reforms. Many Spaniards feared their country might go the way of Portugal, where a leftist revolution has brought political chaos and pushed the nation to the brink of civil war.

Elsewhere, continued conflict between Turkey and Cyprus threatened to wreck the southern flank of the North Atlantic Treaty Organization. In most of Western Europe, interest in common defense reached an all-time low. A sense of danger, so keenly apparent during the Cold War, seemingly evaporated as a result of detente between the United States and Russia.

KEN ALEXANDER
Courtesy San Francisco Examiner

LONDON
AIR
RAID
SHELTER
←

1940

LONDON
IRA
RAID
SHELTER
←

1975

RAY OSRIN
Courtesy Cleveland Plain Dealer

'Now jump down an' play dead !!'

ZSCHIESCHE
KING FEATURES

UNIONS

Britain

BOB ZSCHIESCHE
©King Features

THE KEYS –
GENERALISSIMO
DROP THE KEYS !

JUAN CARLOS

FRANCO SPAIN

DRAPER HILL
Courtesy The Commercial Appeal

GUERNSEY LEPELLEY
Courtesy Christian Science Monitor

OLLIE HARRINGTON
Courtesy New York Daily World

Loose in Portugal

JEFF MACNELLY
Richmond News Leader
©Chicago Tribune—New York
   News Syndicate

"OH GOOD! HERE COMES THE COLONEL NOW.... I BELIEVE WE HAVE A QUORUM."

JAWS

WARREN KING
Courtesy N.Y. Daily News

'It's Part Of Our Deal With Franco—He Wants It Melted Down For Police Bullets'

JACK LANIGAN
Courtesy New Bedford Standard-Times

"FASCISM IS WHEN MAN EXPLOITS MAN...

...COMMUNISM IS THE OTHER WAY AROUND."

"I shouldn't have granted you independence!
You're obviously not ready for self-government."

. . . And Other Issues

The major story on space exploration in 1975 was the Apollo-Soyuz mission in which three American astronauts linked up their vehicle with that of two Soviet cosmonauts some 140 miles above the earth. It was the world's first international hookup in space, and it marked the end of America's manned space ventures until 1978.

In a dramatic warning to the world, Nobel Prize-winner Alexander Solzhenitsyn laid bare the crimes and excesses of his native Russia. He denounced the United States and other Western nations for "the senseless process of endless concessions to aggressors" in the Kremlin.

In April former secretary of the treasury John B. Connally was acquitted of charges of accepting an illegal payoff of $10,000. The verdict seemed to free Connally, a former Democrat turned Republican, for a possible run at the presidency.

THE GREAT AMERICAN BABY-SITTER

BOB PALMER
SPRINGFIELD (MO.) LEADER-PRESS
3-10-75

BOB PALMER
Courtesy Springfield (Mo.)
Leader-Press

A Shot That Shocked the Nation

CY HUNGERFORD
Courtesy Pittsburgh Post-Gazette

TOM FLANNERY
Courtesy Baltimore Sun

'Commercialization is coming, commercialization is coming!'

BOB ARTLEY
Courtesy Worthington (Minn.) Daily Globe

Another sort of bicentennial

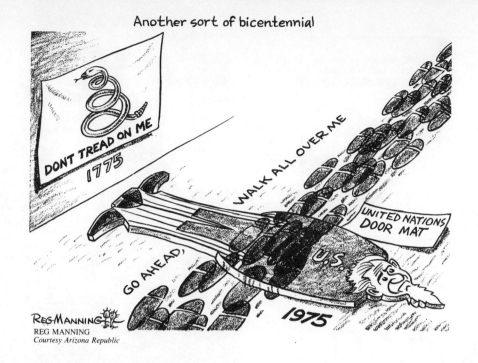

REG MANNING
Courtesy Arizona Republic

200 YEARS OF PROGRESS

JIM LANGE
The Daily Oklahoman
©The Oklahoma Publishing Co.

TOM DARCY
Newsday
©Los Angeles Times Syndicate

"In the nick of time, Myrtle . . . They'll have to put us back"

GUERNSEY LEPELLEY
Courtesy Christian Science Monitor

ROBERT GRAYSMITH
Courtesy San Francisco Chronicle

"Even with his little red book a best seller he's remained his same sweet self . . ."

INTERNATIONAL WOMEN'S CONFERENCE

MIKE PETERS
Courtesy Dayton Daily News

TONY AUTH
Philadelphia Enquirer
©Washington Post Writers' Group

'What are we planning for the Bicentennial?'

EUGENE PAYNE
Courtesy WSOC-TV, Charlotte

Ashville to Salisbury train discontinued

BRICKMAN
©Washington Star Syndicate
and King Features

EDDIE GERMANO
Courtesy Brockton Daily Enterprise

JIM IVEY
Orlando Sentinel Star
©Rothco Cartoons, Inc.

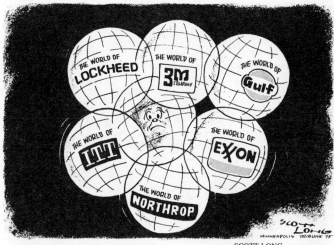

. . . and on the farm they raise some grass . . .
E–I–E–I–O

HERC FICKLEN
Courtesy Dallas Morning News

SPLIT VISIONS

SCOTT LONG
Courtesy Minneapolis Tribune

PA. COURT ORDERS ALL SPORTS OPEN TO GIRLS ....

LLOYD DAVIES
Courtesy Davies Cartoon Service

FRANK INTERLANDI
©Los Angeles Times Syndicate

Mt. Everest conquered by a woman

LEONARD NORRIS
Courtesy Vancouver (Can.) Sun

"Well, he said it's Brotherhood Week . . . I said why not Sisterhood Week, and he said . . ."

Past Award Winners

PULITZER PRIZE
EDITORIAL CARTOON

1922—Rollin Kirby, New York World
1924—J. N. Darling, New York Herald Tribune
1925—Rollin Kirby, New York World
1926—D. R. Fitzpatrick, St. Louis Post-Dispatch
1927—Nelson Harding, Brooklyn Eagle
1928—Nelson Harding, Brooklyn Eagle
1929—Rollin Kirby, New York World
1930—Charles Macauley, Brooklyn Eagle
1931—Edmund Duffy, Baltimore Sun
1932—John T. McCutcheon, Chicago Tribune
1933—H. M. Talburt, Washington Daily News
1934—Edmund Duffy, Baltimore Sun
1935—Ross A. Lewis, Milwaukee Journal
1937—C. D. Batchelor, New York Daily News
1938—Vaughn Shoemaker, Chicago Daily News
1939—Charles G. Werner, Daily Oklahoman
1940—Edmund Duffy, Baltimore Sun
1941—Jacob Burck, Chicago Times
1942—Herbert L. Block, Newspaper Enterprise Association
1943—Jay N. Darling, New York Herald Tribune
1944—Clifford K. Berryman, Washington Star
1945—Bill Mauldin, United Feature Syndicate
1946—Bruce Russell, Los Angeles Times
1947—Vaughn Shoemaker, Chicago Daily News
1948—Reuben L. (Rube) Goldberg, New York Sun
1949—Lute Pease, Newark Evening News
1950—James T. Berryman, Washington Star
1951—Reginald W. Manning, Arizona Republic
1952—Fred L. Packer, New York Mirror
1953—Edward D. Kuekes, Cleveland Plain Dealer
1954—Herbert L. Block, Washington Post
1955—Daniel R. Fitzpatrick, St. Louis Post-Dispatch
1956—Robert York, Louisville Times
1957—Tom Little, Nashville Tennessean
1958—Bruce M. Shanks, Buffalo Evening News
1959—Bill Mauldin, St. Louis Post-Dispatch
1961—Carey Orr, Chicago Tribune
1962—Edmund S. Valtman, Hartford Times

1963—Frank Miller, Des Moines Register
1964—Paul Conrad, Denver Post
1966—Don Wright, Miami News
1967—Patrick B. Oliphant, Denver Post
1968—Eugene Gray Payne, Charlotte Observer
1969—John Fischetti, Chicago Daily News
1970—Thomas F. Darcy, Newsday
1971—Paul Conrad, Los Angeles Times
1972—Jeffrey K. MacNelly, Richmond News Leader
1974—Paul Szep, Boston Globe
1975—Garry Trudeau, Universal Press Syndicate

NOTE: Pulitzer Prize Award was not given
1923, 1936, 1960, 1965, and 1973.

SIGMA DELTA CHI AWARDS
EDITORIAL CARTOON

1942—Jacob Burck, Chicago Times
1943—Charles Werner, Chicago Sun
1944—Henry Barrow, Associated Press
1945—Reuben L. Goldberg, New York Sun
1946—Dorman H. Smith, Newspaper Enterprise Association
1947—Bruce Russell, Los Angeles Times
1948—Herbert Block, Washington Post
1949—Herbert Block, Washington Post
1950—Bruce Russell, Los Angeles Times
1951—Herbert Block, Washington Post, and Bruce Russell, Los
          Angeles Times
1952—Cecil Jensen, Chicago Daily News
1953—John Fischetti, Newspaper Enterprise Association
1954—Calvin Alley, Memphis Commercial Appeal
1955—John Fischetti, Newspaper Enterprise Association
1956—Herbert Block, Washington Post
1957—Scott Long, Minneapolis Tribune
1958—Clifford H. Baldowski, Atlanta Constitution
1959—Charles G. Brooks, Birmingham News
1960—Dan Dowling, New York Herald-Tribune
1961—Frank Interlandi, Des Moines Register
1962—Paul Conrad, Denver Post
1963—William Mauldin, Chicago Sun-Times
1964—Charles Bissell, Nashville Tennessean
1965—Roy Justus, Minneapolis Star
1966—Patrick Oliphant, Denver Post
1967—Eugene Payne, Charlotte Observer
1968—Paul Conrad, Los Angeles Times
1969—William Mauldin, Chicago Sun-Times
1970—Paul Conrad, Los Angeles Times

PAST AWARD WINNERS

1971—Hugh Haynie, Louisville Courier-Journal
1972—William Mauldin, Chicago Sun-Times
1973—Paul Szep, Boston Globe
1974—Mike Peters, Dayton Daily News

NATIONAL HEADLINERS CLUB AWARDS
EDITORIAL CARTOON

1938—C. D. Batchelor, New York Daily News
1939—John Knott, Dallas News
1940—Herbert Block, Newspaper Enterprise Association
1941—Charles H. Sykes, Philadelphia Evening Ledger
1942—Jerry Doyle, Philadelphia Record
1943—Vaughn Shoemaker, Chicago Daily News
1944—Roy Justus, Sioux City Journal
1945—F. O. Alexander, Philadelphia Bulletin
1946—Hank Barrow, Associated Press
1947—Cy Hungerford, Pittsburgh Post-Gazette
1948—Tom Little, Nashville Tennessean
1949—Bruce Russell, Los Angeles Times
1950—Dorman Smith, Newspaper Enterprise Association
1951—C. G. Werner, Indianapolis Star
1952—John Fischetti, Newspaper Enterprise Association
1953—James T. Berryman and Gib Crockett, Washington Star
1954—Scott Long, Minneapolis Tribune
1955—Leo Thiele, Los Angeles Mirror-News
1956—John Milt Morris, Associated Press
1957—Frank Miller, Des Moines Register
1958—Burris Jenkins, Jr., New York Journal-American
1959—Karl Hubenthal, Los Angeles Examiner
1960—Don Hesse, St. Louis Globe-Democrat
1961—L. D. Warren, Cincinnati Enquirer
1962—Franklin Morse, Los Angeles Mirror
1963—Charles Bissell, Nashville Tennessean
1964—Lou Grant, Oakland Tribune
1965—Merle R. Tingley, London (Ont.) Free Press
1966—Hugh Haynie, Louisville Courier-Journal
1967—Jim Berry, Newspaper Enterprise Association
1968—Warren King, New York News
1969—Larry Barton, Toledo Blade
1970—Bill Crawford, Newspaper Enterprise Association
1971—Ray Osrin, Cleveland Plain Dealer
1972—Jacob Burck, Chicago Sun-Times
1973—Ranan Lurie, New York Times
1974—Tom Darcy, Newsday
1975—Bill Sanders, Milwaukee Journal

NATIONAL NEWSPAPER
AWARD/CANADA

1949—Jack Boothe, Toronto Globe and Mail
1950—James G. Reidford, Montreal Star
1951—Len Norris, Vancouver Sun
1952—Robert La Palme, Le Devoir, Montreal
1953—Robert W. Chambers, Halifax Chronicle-Herald
1954—John Collins, Montreal Gazette
1955—Merle R. Tingley, London Free Press
1956—James G. Reidford, Toronto Globe and Mail
1957—James G. Reidford, Toronto Globe and Mail
1958—Raoul Hunter, Le Soleil, Quebec
1959—Duncan Macpherson, Toronto Star
1960—Duncan Macpherson, Toronto Star
1961—Ed McNally, Montreal Star
1962—Duncan Macpherson, Toronto Star
1963—Jan Kamienski, Winnipeg Tribune
1964—Ed McNally, Montreal Star
1965—Duncan Macpherson, Toronto Star
1966—Robert W. Chambers, Halifax Chronicle-Herald
1967—Raoul Hunter, Le Soleil, Quebec
1968—Roy Peterson, Vancouver Sun
1969—Edward Uluschak, Edmonton Journal
1970—Duncan Macpherson, Toronto Daily Star
1971—Yardley Jones, Toronto Sun
1972—Duncan Macpherson, Toronto Star
1973—John Collins, Montreal Gazette
1974—Blaine, Hamilton Spectator

Index

INDEX